YOUR KNOWLEDGE HAS

Bibliographic information published by the German National Library:

The German National Library lists this publication in the National Bibliography; detailed bibliographic data are available on the Internet at http://dnb.dnb.de .

Imprint:

Copyright © 2017 GRIN Verlag, Open Publishing GmbH
Print and binding: Books on Demand GmbH, Norderstedt Germany
ISBN: 9783668493940

This book at GRIN:

http://www.grin.com/en/e-book/371131/statistical-analysis-of-the-gsm-global-system-for-mobile-communications

Vincent Nyangaresi, Silvance Abeka, Solomon Ogara

Statistical analysis of the GSM (Global System for Mobile Communications) mobility prediction models

GRIN Publishing

GRIN - Your knowledge has value

Since its foundation in 1998, GRIN has specialized in publishing academic texts by students, college teachers and other academics as e-book and printed book. The website www.grin.com is an ideal platform for presenting term papers, final papers, scientific essays, dissertations and specialist books.

Visit us on the internet:

http://www.grin.com/

http://www.facebook.com/grincom

http://www.twitter.com/grin_com

STATISTICAL ANALYSIS OF THE GSM MOBILITY PREDICTION MODELS

Vincent O. Nyangaresi[1]

(Student, Information Technology Security & Audit)

Silvance O. Abeka[2]

(Dean, School Of Informatics and Innovative Systems)

Solomon O. Ogara[3]

(Chairman, Department of Computer Science & Software Engineering)

Jaramogi Oginga Odinga University of Science & Technology

July, 2017

Abstract

In the GSM environment, mobility prediction is concerned with envisaging of the mobile station's next movement. By accurately employing the predicted movement, the GSM network is capable of attaining enhanced resource allocation and reservations, better assignment of cells to location areas, more efficient paging, and call admission control. Numerous studies have been carried out in mobile station prediction and as such, many mobility predictions have been developed. The goal of this paper was to statistically analyze these mobility prediction models in order to understand their strengths and weaknesses. The results of this analysis indicated that the current mobility models base their predictions on movement patterns of users throughout physical space. However, they do not directly relate to movement throughout the network based on the cell presently hosting a mobile station. In addition, several base transceiver stations may overlap over a single physical location, a complication not captured by the current mobility prediction models. Therefore, there is need for a generic mobility prediction model that can depict movement of mobile users more realistically within the GSM network coverage areas. As such, this paper proposes the development of a mobility prediction model that is capable of accurately reflecting mobile station movement in real-world cellular networks, taking into consideration the actual scenarios such as base transceiver stations overlapping. The requirements for this novel mobility prediction model are also provided, and were based on the shortcomings noted in the existing mobility prediction models. The significance of the proposed model lies on the fact that in order to   pre-allocate resources for seamless connectivity during handovers, the mobility prediction model should anticipate the actual cell that the mobile station will next connect to, rather than the physical location they will move to.

Keywords: *GSM, Mobile station, Mobility prediction*

Table of Content

Abstract.. 2

PART I.. 6

GSM CELLULAR COMMUNICATIONS.. 6

    1.1 Preamble 6

    1.2 Significance of Mobility Prediction.. 7

PART II 9

GSM MOBILITY PREDICTION MODELS... 9

    2.1 Introduction.. 9

    2.2 Obstacle Mobility Model 9

    2.3 Street Unit Model.. 9

    2.4 City Area Mobility Model 9

    2.5 Random Walk Model... 10

    2.6 Random Waypoint Model.. 10

    2.7 Markovian Random Walk 10

    2.8 Random Direction Model 10

    2.9 Shortest Path Model... 11

    2.10 Normal Walk Models... 11

    2.11 Smooth Random Mobility Model 11

    2.12 Microscopic Models.. 11

    2.13 Mesoscopic Models 12

    2.14 Macroscopic Models... 12

    2.15 Reference Point Group Mobility... 13

    2.16 Column Mobility Model 13

    2.17 Pursue Mobility Model 14

    2.18 Nomadic Community Mobility Model 14

    2.19 Activity-Based Model... 14

    2.20 Cell-Residence-Time-Based Model.. 14

    2.21 Pathway Mobility.. 15

PART III 16

MOBILITY TAXONOMY ARCHITECTURE 16

    3.1 Introduction 16

    3.2 Taxonomy Development 16

    3.3 Taxonomy Parameters 19

PART IV 21

GSM MOBILITY MODELS PARAMETRIC ANALYSIS 21

    4.1 Introduction 21

    4.2 Models Based On Location and Fixed Velocity 21

    4.3 High Probability Prediction Models 23

    4.4 Cell to Cell Mobility Models 25

    4.5 Models Based On Feasible Future Sequence of Cells 27

    4.6 Models Based On Degree Of Randomness 28

        4.6.1 Trace-Based Models 28

        4.6.2 Constrained Topology Models 29

        4.6.3 Statistical Models 30

    4.7 Models Based On Level of Description 36

        4.7.1 Fluid Flow Model 36

        4.7.2 Gravity Mobility Models 36

    4.8 Models Based On Individual User Behaviors 37

    4.9 Models Based On Nodes Movement Dependency 38

        4.9.1 Temporal Dependency of Velocity 38

        4.9.2 Spatial Dependency of Velocity 38

    4.10 Models Based On Real Network Movement Depiction 40

PART V 41

CRITIC OF GSM MOBILITY PREDICTION MODELS 41

    5.1 Introduction 41

    5.2 Models Based On Location and Fixed Velocity 41

    5.3 Models Based On High Probability Prediction 42

    5.4 Cell to Cell Mobility Models 42

    5.5 Models Based On Feasible Future Sequence of Cells 42

    5.6 Models Based On Degree of Randomness 43

5.7 Models Based On Level of Description 45

5.8 Models Based On Individual User Behaviors 45

5.9 Models Based On Nodes Movement Dependency 46

5.10 Models Based On Real Network Movement Depiction 46

PART VI 47

PROPOSED MOBILITY PREDICTION MODEL 47

6.1 Introduction 47

6.2 Requirements for the Proposed Model 47

Conclusions 48

REFERENCES 49

PART I

GSM CELLULAR COMMUNICATIONS

1.1 Preamble

The emergences of information technology and telecommunication services have had a huge impact in people's day to day lives. Globally, each and every sector of people's economic, social and cultural lives has been affected by these technologies. In particular, mobile communication services have been accepted as part of office procedure. An increasing number of organizations are allowing their employees to utilize their mobile stations to carry out office work, a concept referred to as Bring Your Own Device (BYUOD). In the homes, mobile stations are crucial in keeping in touch with family members. Effective mobile communication requires an accurate mobility prediction model so that network services can be delivered to them without long network paging delays.

As Mona et al., (2015) found out, mobile communication services have led to some security concerns. This owes to the increased flexibility that allows criminals to commit crime from one location and move virtually to other locations and still enjoy perfect cellular communications. Terrorists are also increasingly using mobile communication services to coordinate their activities. Any effort towards counter-terrorism or crime prevention requires that there be a more efficient geographical location management scheme so that law enforcement departments can track the culprits with increased precision.

As a result of the huge uptake of mobile communication services, most GSM networks can be easily overwhelmed with traffic data. In highly populated locations such as cities, chances of connection delays, numbers of uncompleted and dropped calls are common scenarios (Abdou et al., 2015). This can be attributed to the problems that are inherent in the present process of updating and searching the current locations of multiple mobile nodes in a GSM network.

The challenges outlined above all stem from the fact that the current mobility prediction models are not effective enough to provide an accurate depiction of the actual mobile user movements within the GSM coverage area. This paper sought to unravel the statistical genesis of these mobility models shortcomings.

1.2 Significance of Mobility Prediction

The ultimate goal of the GSM mobility prediction models is to make an attempt in imitating the movement of real mobile stations, which are characterized by the change of speed and direction with time (Petteri, 2016). This allows the network to track the location where the subscribers are currently residing. In so doing these mobility modes permit voice calls, short messages (SMS), general packet radio services (GPRS) and other mobile phone services to be delivered to the subscribers.

According to Nweke et al., (2015), mobility prediction models are significant in the provision and maintenance of communication with a mobile user at any given point in time. This is particularly true now that there has been a growing trend of the convergence of numerous financial services such as banking applications with mobile communication services. However, with the swift growth in the number of mobile subscribers globally, mobility prediction has emerged as one of the most important and challenging tasks for mobile communication systems.

The mobility management enables the serving network to locate a mobile subscriber's point of attachment for delivery of data packets, and maintenance of a mobile station's connection as it continues to change its point of attachment (Nandeppanavar et al., 2010). However, with the amalgamation of data traffic on GSM networks coupled with the increasing demand for improved throughput and security, mobile station movement prediction has become a serious concern.

In their study, Garud et al., (2015) indicated that mobility prediction is an important factor contributing to the overall performance of mobile telecommunication networks. This is due to its ability of restraining the ability of the GSM network in maintaining a connection or guarantying a quality of service among the subscribers. In addition, the ever increasing number of telecommunication customers has radically increased the consequences of poor mobility prediction on network maintenance.

Patle and Sanjay (2016) discuss that due to the significance of mobility prediction, several studies have been conducted and their results have led to the development of a number of mobility prediction models such as random waypoint, random walk, random Markovian walk, random direction mobility, smooth random mobility, cell-residence-time-based, Gauss–Markov, Fluid Flow, normal walk, shortest path, activity-based, pursue mobility, nomadic community mobility, reference point group mobility(in-place mobility, overlap mobility, convention mobility), Manhattan grid, pathway mobility, obstacle mobility, Freeway mobility, Street Unit, Street Pattern Tracing, mobility vector, gravity models, city section mobility, city area mobility, First order Kinetic, Feynman-Verlet, Semi-Hidden Markov, Autoregressive (AR), Global Mobility among others.

The rest of this paper is organized as follows: Part II provides a review of the current GSM mobility prediction models while Part III explains the developed taxonomy for the GSM mobile stations mobility prediction models. Part IV carries out some parametric analysis of the mobility prediction models whereas Part V offers a critic of the models. Lastly, Part VI presents the requirements for an ideal GSM mobility prediction model and the conclusion that can be draw from this study.

PART II

GSM MOBILITY PREDICTION MODELS

2.1 Introduction

According to Chuyen et al., (2014), numerous mobile station prediction models have been developed to assist in the forecasting of mobile stations movement patterns within the network coverage area. The most common ones are discussed in the following sub-sections.

2.2 Obstacle Mobility Model

In this model, mobile station mobility is depicted by taking into consideration real-life scenarios such as the fact that people move towards specific destinations rather than randomly choosing some destinations; obstacles such a buildings, parks or rivers can block people's movements as well hinder signal propagation; and that people do not walk along random directions but along pathways and select shortest paths (Aarti et al., 2012).

2.3 Street Unit Model

Here, the mobile station is permitted to move on a rectangular, Manhattan grid only, where the grid depicts the street pattern of suburban or urban areas. The mobile station speed is selected from a normal distribution and is updated periodically or can be area dependent. Tarik et al., (2011) discuss that direction changes can occur at every crossroads, where the probabilities can be different for each of the four possible directions at every crossroads. Furthermore, other models can be considered in this point due to their comparable characteristics with Street Unit Model, such as *high-way traffic models*. These models are able to describe the mobility behaviour of mobile stations with an accuracy of a few meters, and hence are useful for devising efficient and effective dynamic channel assignment algorithms.

2.4 City Area Mobility Model

This model is utilized to describe mobile station mobility and traffic behaviour within a city area environment. The transport theory states that although each individual city area exhibits specific characteristics, they share generic features that can be considered as assumptions for representing mobile station's movement. The first assumption is that the population density gradually decreases as one shifts towards the city edges in suburban and rural area. Biju et al., (2010) point out that on the contrary, densely populated areas surround the city centre with high density of workplaces and shopping centers. The second conjecture is that the street network supports two movement types, radial and peripheral. The last postulation is that the geographical area covers the whole city area, consisting of a set of zones connected via high capacity routes. A zone is regarded as corresponding to a network area, such as macro cell and streets are regarded as high capacity routes. The stochastic part corresponds to the mobile station mobility behavior such as initial distribution, type of movement, criterion for selecting routes, and traffic behavior exampled by call arrival rates and available services.

2.5 Random Walk Model

This is an individual mobility model that is memory-less since it does not retain knowledge related to its past speed and direction. Consequently, the mobile station future velocity is independent of the current velocity (Patle and Sanjay, 2016).

2.6 Random Waypoint Model

Rogerio and Roberto (2016) discuss that this is a simple stochastic model in which a mobile station moves on a restricted continuous plane from its current position to a new location by randomly choosing its destination coordinates, its speed of movement, and the amount of time that it will pause on arriving at the destination.

2.7 Markovian Random Walk

This is a modified form of the random walk model that utilizes Markov chains to describe the mobile station movement, and it introduces memory in the movement behavior of the mobile station (Rong-Hua et al., 2015). Also referred to as the probabilistic version of the random walk model, this model employs three states to represent the movement coordinates x and y: state zero (0) represents the current position of the mobile station; state one (1) represents the previous position of the mobile station; while state two (2) represents the next position of the mobile station.

2.8 Random Direction Model

This model is similar to the Random Waypoint Model, only that instead of choosing a destination, the mobile station randomly selects a direction from a given interval and moves in that direction (Jogendra and Panda, 2016). After some random time taken from an exponential distribution, the user either changes direction or changes speed. The movement can occur freely anywhere in the network coverage area. The values for the direction are taken from a uniform distribution on the interval $[0, 2\pi]$ and the values for the speed follow a uniform distribution or a normal distribution.

2.9 Shortest Path Model

This model is utilized to represent the mobility of vehicular mobile stations. It assumes that within the location area, a mobile station follows the shortest path measured in the number of cells passed through, from source to destination. According to Swati and Hina (2014), at each intersection, the mobile station makes a decision to proceed to any of the neighboring cells such that the shortest distance assumption is maintained.

2.10 Normal Walk Models

This is straight-oriented mobility model referred which assumes that a mobile station moves in unit steps on a Euclidean plane (Hala, 2015). In this model, the next movement direction is chosen from a normal distribution with zero mean.

2.11 Smooth Random Mobility Model

This is an enhanced random mobility model that makes the movement trace of individual mobile stations more realistic than common approaches for random movement (Logambal and Chitra, 2016). In this model, the movement pattern is based on random processes for speed and direction control in which new values are correlated to the previous ones. Upon a speed change incident, a new target speed is selected, and acceleration is set to achieve this target speed. The principles for the direction changes are also similar to those of the speed change.

2.12 Microscopic Models

These models depict the movement of a single mobile station by its space and speed coordinates at a given time t. The goal here is to obtain a very detailed representation for one entity within the network coverage area. Such models include *Street Unit Models* and *Street Pattern Tracing Models*. In the former, the mobile station is permitted to move on a rectangular grid only. Both the Manhattan and freeway models fall in this group. Joanne (2014) explains that in the latter models, the mobile station is allowed to move on a predefined stretch only. As such, they are good at depicting movements along highways or main streets where directions changes are very unlikely to occur. In these models, only the speed v of a mobile station is selected randomly from a uniform or normal distribution. The direction is given by the position of the mobile station within the highway or street. At an intersection of a horizontal and a vertical street, the mobile station can turn left, right or go straight with certain probability. This model is therefore ideal for mimicking the motion pattern of mobile stations on streets defined by maps.

2.13 Mesoscopic Models

These models depict the homogenized movement behaviour of several mobile stations instead of only one. Daniel et al., (2016) point out that here, the mobile users shift as groups (hence group models). Examples of these models include *Reference Point Group Mobility* (In-Place Mobility, Overlap Mobility, and Convention Mobility) and *Mobility Vector model*. The goal here is to derive a distribution function of the number of vehicles at a certain location (x, y) or speed v in order to describe the movement of the group. In these models, each mobile station has a logical centre and the trajectory of the group as a whole is represented by the locus of the centre. Though each mobile station has its own reference point, the group moves as a single entity because the reference points follow the group movement. *In-place mobility*, a given geographical area is partitioned such that each and every subset of the original area is allocated to a specific group, and each group operates only within their geographic subset. It is therefore ideal for simulating scenarios in which groups of people, that have similar goals, are assigned to restricted areas. For the case of *Overlap Mobility*, several different groups, each of them having diverse tasks, working in the same geographic area are described. Here, each group may have varying characteristics compared with other groups within the same geographical boundary. In *Convention Mobility*, both the conference attendees and the revelations are represented. In addition, different revelations are housed in different rooms and the rooms are connected to facilitate travel between exhibits. Moreover, this model partitions a given area into smaller subsets and permits the groups to move in a similar pattern throughout each subset.

2.14 Macroscopic Models

In these models, Fabrício et al., (2015) elaborate, the focus is on density, mean speed, speed variance, and traffic flow of vehicles. Examples of these models include *fluid flow models*, *gravity models* and the *random walk models*.

A. Fluid Flow Model:

This model is employed to investigate the average number of mobile stations crossing a boundary of a network coverage area. Tao et al., (2016) discuss that it derives from transportation theory and describes the movement of a group of users. As such, the *Reference Point Group Model* is included in this family. It can be employed for both intra-cell and inter-cell movements of mobile stations. It works by averaging the mobility patterns of all mobiles stations and as such, it is often used to describe the aggregate mobility behavior of all mobile stations.

A. Gravity Mobility Models

These models are also derived from transportation theory and they give an aggregated description of the movement of several users, as was the case for the fluid model. They are based on Newton's gravitational law and spatial interactions such as attractiveness and repulsiveness among the mobile stations (Mariano at al., 2016). In Newton's gravity model, the movement of a mobile station from a given point to another is directly proportional to the attraction of the area and inversely proportional to the distance of separation between them.

C. Random Walk Models

These models depict the movement of individual mobile stations from cell to cell. According to Adebiyi et al., (2016), a state transition diagram defines this model, in which a cell is represented by a state and the mobile station movement is represented by transition probabilities between the states. As such, these models are interested in the cell where the mobile station resides and not its exact location.

2.15 Reference Point Group Mobility

In this model, each group has a center that can be either a logical center or a group leader mobile station. Here, each group is made up of one leader and a number of members (Jaswant and Rajneesh, 2016). The movement of the group leader influences the mobility behavior of the entire group.

2.16 Column Mobility Model

This is utilized to describe a set of mobile stations such as robots moving in a certain fixed direction. As Ahmad (2016) explains, it can be employed in searching and scanning activity, such as destroying mines by military robots.

2.17 Pursue Mobility Model

This mimics scenarios where several mobile stations endeavor to capture single mobile station ahead. As such, it could be utilized in target tracking and law enforcement. Here, the mobile station being pursued serves as the target mobile station and it moves freely in accordance with the Random Waypoint model (Kim et al., 2017). The pursuer mobile stations direct their velocity towards the position of the targeted mobile station in an attempt to intercept it.

2.18 Nomadic Community Mobility Model

This model serves to symbolize the mobility scenarios where a group of mobile stations travel together and can therefore be applied to depict mobile communication in a conference or military application. Mostafa (2016) expound that in this model, the entire group of mobile stations shifts randomly from one location to another and the reference point of each mobile station is established based on the common movement of this group.

2.19 Activity-Based Model

In activity-based model, instead of using a set of random variables to depict the mobility pattern, it is assumed that a trip is undertaken for participating in an activity such as shopping at a given destination. Martin et al., (2016) illustrate that once the location for the next activity has been determined, the route from the current location to this activity location is computed in terms of cells traversed.

2.20 Cell-Residence-Time-Based Model

The idea here is to establish the connection time spent by a mobile station within one location. According to Chuyen et al., (2014), this requires the tracing of the movement of individual users. In their paper, Yi-Bing et al., (2011) used the standard counter values such as the number of handovers and call traffic measured in a mobile telecommunications network to derive the cell residence times. However, measurement of cell residence times in a commercially operated mobile network is not trivial.

2.21 Pathway Mobility

In this model, geographic constraints are integrated into the mobility model by restricting the mobile station movement to the pathways in the map. In these maps, the vertices represent the buildings of the city, and the edges depict the streets and freeways between these buildings. Mahmoud et al., (2016) discuss that initially, the mobile stations are randomly positioned on the edges of the graph and then for each mobile station, a destination is selected arbitrarily and the mobile station moves towards this destination via the shortest path along the edges. On arrival at the destination, the mobile station pauses for T_{pause} time and again chooses a new destination for the next movement.

This procedure is repeated until the end of simulation. The mobile stations in this model are only permitted to travel on the pathways. However, since the destination of each motion phase is haphazardly selected, a certain level of randomness still exists for this model. As such, in this graph based mobility model, the mobile stations move in a pseudo-random fashion on the pathways

PART III

MOBILITY TAXONOMY ARCHITECTURE

3.1 Introduction

The aim of this paper was to statistically analyze the current mobility prediction models in order to gain in-depth understanding of their limitations in as far as the provision of precise mobile station movement is concerned. As such, a parametric analysis of mobility prediction criteria was carried out first for the models under study to determine the constructs and the computations involved during the mobility prediction process.

3.2 Taxonomy Development

Based on the similarity of these constructs and computations involved, this paper developed a taxonomy for mobility prediction models that placed these models in their precise categories as follows: Location and Fixed Velocity (LFV), High Probability Prediction (HPP); Cell to Cell Mobility (CCM); Feasible Future Sequence of Cells (FFSC); Degree Of Randomness (DOR); Level of Description (LD); Individual User Behaviors (IUB); Nodes Movement Dependency (NMD); and Real Network Movement Depiction (RNMD). Figure 1 gives a pictorial representation of this taxonomy.

As this figure shows, they were four models based on location and fixed velocity (LFV), which included *freeway mobility, Manhattan grid mobility, Feynman-Verlet mobility* and *first order kinetic* models. These models were statistically investigated using position, velocity and acceleration. The high prediction probability (HPP) was the second taxonomic group consisting of three models namely semi-hidden *Markov, autoregressive* and *Gauss-Markov* models. These models were concerned with correct prediction of the mobile station position with high probability and hence were analyzed using Markov-Gaussian process, probability, velocity, auto-correlation and variance.

The third taxonomy was cell to cell mobility (CCM) that consisted of three models: *global mobility prediction, Neuro-fuzzy inference* and *shadow cluster*. These models dealt with User Mobility Patterns (UMP) and User Actual Path (UAP) and hence were analyzed using cell and position profiles for each mobile station. The next category was that of models based on feasible future sequence of

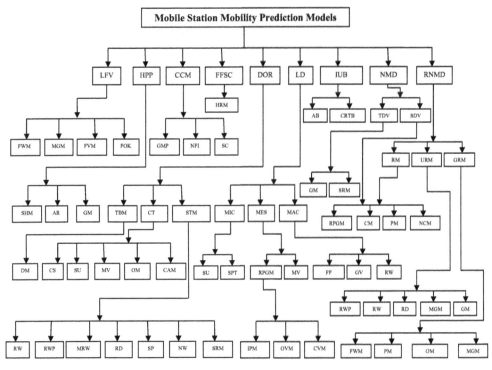

LEGEND

FWM : Freeway Mobility	**MV** : Mobility Vector	**IPM** : In-Place Mobility
MGM : Manhattan Grid Mobility	**OM** : Obstacle Mobility	**OVM** : Overlap Mobility
FVM : Feynman-Verlet Mobility	**CAM** : City Area Mobility	**CVM** : Conventional Mobility
FOK : First order kinetic	**RW** : Random Walk	**FF** : Fluid Flow
SHM : Semi-Hidden Markov	**RWP** : Random Waypoint	**GVM** : Gravity Mobility
AR : Autoregressive	**MRK** : Markovian Random Walk	**AB** : Activity –Based
GM : Gauss-Markov	**RD** : Random Direction	**CRTB** : Cell-Residence Time Based
GMP : Global Mobility Prediction	**SP** : Shortest Path	**TDV** : Temporal Dependency on Velocity
NFI : Neuro-Fuzzy Inference	**NW** : Normal Walk	**SDV** : Spatial Dependency on Velocity
SC : Shadow Cluster	**SRM** : Smooth Random Mobility	**CM** : Column Mobility
HRM : Hierarchical Mobility	**SPT** : Street Pattern Tracing	**PM** : Pursue Mobility
TBM : Trace Based Mobility	**MIC** : Microscopic	**NCM** : Nomadic Community Model
CT : Constrained Topology	**MES** : Mesoscopic	**RM** : Realistic Mobility
STM : Statistical Mobility	**MAC** : Macroscopic	**URM** : Unrealistic Mobility
DM : Deterministic Mobility	**RPGM** : Reference Point Group Mobility	**GRM** : Geographically Restricted Mobility
CS : City Section		**PM** : Path Mobility
SU : Street Unit		

Figure 1: Taxonomy of Mobility Prediction Models

cells that a mobile station will visit and consisted of *hierarchical mobility* models. As such, the analysis here was accomplished using correlation area of the neighboring cells, distance between mobile station and the base transceiver station, direction of motion, bearing of cell vertex, and the cell-crossing probability.

For the fifth category, the degree of randomness (DOR) for the mobile station movement process was employed and the models here were: *trace-based mobility, constrained mobility* and *statistical mobility*. The constructs and computations involved in these models consisted of velocity, amplitude, angular frequency, phase angle, vectors, Voronoi diagrams, directions, Markov chains, state transition probability, Gaussian distribution, pause time, probability density function, graphs, acceleration, and weighted edges. Models utilizing level of description (LD) were *microscopic, mesoscopic* and *macroscopic*. Here, direction, amount of traffic flow out of a region, population density within the region, attractivity of the location, average velocity, and the length of the region boundary were involved in the mobility prediction process.

Actual user activities at a destination and the amount of time spent in a given cell are parameters required for mobility prediction in individual user behavior (IUB) based models. Such models include activity-based and cell residence time based models. For the case of Nodes Movement Dependency, the mobile station movement is influenced by that of other mobile stations within the coverage area. This dependency can be in form of temporal dependency of velocity or spatial dependency of velocity. As such, parameters of interest here include group leader velocity, individual mobile station velocity, motion vector, maximum allowed distance deviation, advance vector, previous reference point, reference grid, mobile station position, and projected position of target.

In the last taxonomical unit of Real Network Movement Depiction (RNMD), examples of models here include realistic mobility, unrealistic mobility and geographically restricted mobility. The parameters and computations required here are individual mobile station velocity, Voronoi diagrams, direction of motion, projected position of target, maximum allowed distance deviation group leader velocity, motion vector, advance vector, previous reference point, reference grid, and mobile station position.

3.3 Taxonomy Parameters

It was noted that for a particular taxonomy of mobility model, a number of parameters were utilized as inputs to direction and movement magnitude computations. Table 1 gives a summary of the taxonomical units, parameters involved and the kind of computations carried out to facilitate mobility prediction.

Table 1: Parameters and Required Computations for Various Taxonomical Units

Taxonomical Unit	Parameters	Computations
LFV	Position, velocity, acceleration, maximum transmission range	Kinetic distance between mobile station locations, position predictions
HPP	Gaussian random variable, previous value of velocity, memory level parameter, present velocity, last reported location	Probability, Expectation, auto-correlation and variance.
CCM	User Mobility Patterns, User Actual Path, matching threshold	Pattern-matching, edit distance,
FFSC	Received signal strength indicator, cell geometry, correlation area, direction of motion, bearing of cell vertex	Cell-crossing probability, dynamic state estimation, distance between mobile station and BTS, probability density function
DOR	Velocity, direction of motion, , base vector, acceleration, deviation vector, Voronoi diagrams, vertices, amplitude, angular frequency, phase angle, directions, , Gaussian distribution, pause time, graphs, acceleration, and weighted edges, queue of all nodes, an empty set,	Mobility vector, Markov chains, state transition probability, probability density function, velocity vector, next waypoint, distances from the source mobile station, smallest distance,
LD	Direction, population density within the region, average velocity, position of origin location, location of destination, distance between the location of origin and the location of destination,	Traffic flow out of a region, attractivity of the location, length of the region boundary, number of site crossings per unit time
IUB	Destination, activity performed at destination, connection time spent by a mobile station within one location	Route from the current location to next activity location, Number of cells crossed, traces of the movement of individual users
NMD	Group leader velocity, individual mobile station velocity, maximum allowed distance deviation, advance vector, previous reference point, reference grid, random vector ,	Motion vector of group member, current reference point, projected position of target, mobile station position,
RNMD	Individual mobile station velocity, Voronoi diagrams, direction of motion, , maximum allowed distance deviation group leader velocity, advance vector, previous reference point, reference grid	Projected position of target, motion vector, mobile station position

This table shows that different parameters and computations are performed for each of the nine taxonomical units. The following sub-section delves into the actual computations that are necessary for mobile station mobility prediction.

PART IV

GSM MOBILITY MODELS PARAMETRIC ANALYSIS

4.1 Introduction

In this section, the finer details about the parameters and the actual computations that facilitate mobility prediction in a GSM network are given. It was noted that various prediction models shared input parameters to the mobility prediction process and some computations. As such, it was possible for one prediction model to fit into more than one taxonomical unit as illustrated in the following sub-sections.

4.2 Models Based On Location and Fixed Velocity

The mobility prediction models that concentrate on the position and a fixed velocity of the mobile station are generally deterministic in nature. In these modes, the future values of the mobile station movement can be predicted from the past values. Examples of these models are *Freeway, Manhattan, Feynman-Verlet* and *first order kinetic model*. In these models, the new position Q $(X_{i+1},\ Y_{i+1})$ of mobile stations that were initially at point $P(X,\ Y)$ is computed using (1):

$$\overrightarrow{pos}_{i+1} = \begin{pmatrix} X_{i+1} \\ Y_{i+1} \end{pmatrix} = \begin{pmatrix} X_i \\ Y_i \end{pmatrix} + \begin{pmatrix} v_x^i \\ v_y^i \end{pmatrix} * (t - t_i) \tag{1}$$

In this relation, X and Y are the X-coordinates and Y-coordinates respectively while V_x and V_y are the velocities along the X and Y coordinates respectively. The kinetic distance between these two points P and Q is calculated as illustrated in (2):

$$\left. \begin{aligned} D_{PQ}^2\ (t) &= D_{QP}^2\ (t) = \parallel \overrightarrow{pos}\ _Q\ (t) - \overrightarrow{pos}\ _P\ (t)\parallel_2^2 \\[6pt] &= \left[\begin{pmatrix} X_Q - X_P \\ Y_Q - Y_P \end{pmatrix} + \begin{pmatrix} V_Q^x - V_P^x \\ V_Q^y - V_P^y \end{pmatrix} * t\ \right]^2 \\[6pt] &= aPQt^2 + bPQt + cPQ \end{aligned} \right\} \tag{2}$$

Here, a, b and c are constant. Considering r as the base transceiver station (BTS) maximum transmission range, then as long as the kinetic distance is less or equal to r^2, the mobile node remains within the range of this particular BTS. To compute the time intervals during which the mobile stations are within the BTS control, (3) is utilized:

$$\left.\begin{array}{l} D_{PQ}^2(t) - r^2 = 0 \\ aPQt^2 + bPQt + cPQ - r^2 = 0 \end{array}\right\} \tag{3}$$

However, in practice, the mobile station velocity may be varying as the nodes move within the GSM coverage area. In such cases, a second order prediction model based on the Euler motion law is used as shown in (4):

$$\left.\begin{array}{l} \vec{V}_{i+1} = \vec{a}_i . t + \vec{V}_i \\ \overrightarrow{pos}_{i+1} = \dfrac{1}{2}\vec{a}_i . t^2 + \vec{V}_i t + \overrightarrow{pos}_i \end{array}\right\} \tag{4}$$

In many cases, vehicular motions involve impulsive forces such as sudden braking. However, a constant acceleration is usually accepted in high speed mobility networks. On the contrary, a piecewise constant acceleration is utilized in practice. In both of these cases, (4) may be employed to predict a future position based on some kinetic information. Using substitution method:

$$\left.\begin{array}{l} \overrightarrow{pos}_{i+1} = \dfrac{1}{2}.(\dfrac{\vec{V}_{i+1} - \vec{V}_i}{t}).t^2 + \vec{V}_i.t + \overrightarrow{pos}_i \\ = (\dfrac{\vec{V}_{i+1} + \vec{V}_i}{2}).t + \overrightarrow{pos}_i \end{array}\right\} \tag{5}$$

Equation (5) clearly indicates that position predictions in these models are computed using a velocity one step ahead. This means that two samples of past velocities and two piecewise constant accelerations must be known beforehand in order to predict the future mobile user position.

4.3 High Probability Prediction Models

The aim of these models does not lie on getting an exact prediction of the mobile station position. On the contrary, they focus on obtaining the correct prediction with high probability. This makes them stochastic in nature, and are therefore employed to add an uncertainty element to deterministic predictions models. Examples of these models include *Semi-Hidden Markov, Autoregressive (AR)* and *Gauss-Markov*.

These models are employed to represent anonymous parameters in the state equations or to take into consideration the model's prediction error. It is also probable to utilize these models for both applications.

As an illustration, tracking-based autoregressive processes (AR) make use of the white noise to model the AR prediction errors, and the estimation of the states, exampled by position or velocity, is regularly accomplished using Kalman Filters. In these situations, even if positions or velocities are computed without error, the AR process still provides predictions with some errors.

In cases where errors are added to the states (positions or velocities), the performance normally deteriorates severely. Therefore, joint optimization is applied to obtain good predictions in many practical applications. Here, four approaches including Autoregressive processes, Kalman Filtering, semi-Hidden Markov and semi-Hidden Markov or Particle Filtering are employed for mobility tracking. The two measurements that are normally applied in these models are the Received Signal Strength Indicator (RSSI) and the Time or Arrival (TOA). The first and simplest representation is to weight a deterministic prediction by the probability the prediction still exists, which is defined by (6):

$$Pred^{stoch}(t) = Pred^{det}(t). e^{-\beta(t-t_{sample})} \tag{6}$$

Here, $Pred^{det}(t)$ is the deterministic mobility prediction at time t; $e^{-\beta(t-t_{sample})}$ is the stochastic validity of the prediction parameters; β is the stability of the mobility parameters or predictability; and t_{sample} is the latest sampling time of the mobility parameters.

In the Gauss-Markov prediction model, a mobile station's velocity is first represented as a time-correlated Gauss-Markov random process. In discrete time, this model calculates the predicted velocity depending on the previous value of velocity and a Gaussian process given by (7)

$$v(t) = \alpha v_{t-1} + (1 - \alpha)\mu + \sigma\sqrt{1 - \alpha^2}w_{t-1} \qquad (7)$$

with a Gauss-Markovian auto-correlation process given by (8)

$$R_v(\tau) = E[v(t)v(t + \tau)] = \sigma e^{-\beta|\tau|} + \mu^2 \qquad (8)$$

where, $\alpha = e^{-\beta|\tau|}$; β is the memory size; σ^2 is the variance of the $v(t)$ process; M is the expectation of the $v(t)$ process; and w_t is the Gaussian process.

In this case, t is the discrete unit of time and w_t is an uncorrelated Gaussian process with zero mean and unit variance and is independent of v_t. The memory level parameter α reflects the randomness of the Gauss-Markov process. As the memory level parameter increases, the present velocity is more likely to be influenced by its previous velocity. On the other hand, when the memory level parameter reduces, the current velocity is mainly affected by the Gaussian random variable.

In equations (7) and (8), as α approaches zero, or β approaches infinity, (7) the model represented is a nomadic random walk mobility pattern with mean μ and standard deviation σ. On the other hand, as α approaches one or β approaches zero, (7) represents a constant velocity fluid-flow mobility pattern with $v_n = v_0$ for all n. Relation (7) can be written in two – dimensional (2-D) field as shown in (9):

$$\left.\begin{array}{l} v_t^x = \alpha v_{t-1}^x + (1 - \alpha)v^x + \sigma^x\sqrt{1 - \alpha^2}w_{t-1}^x \\ v_t^y = \alpha v_{t-1}^y + (1 - \alpha)v^y + \sigma^y\sqrt{1 - \alpha^2}w_{t-1}^y \end{array}\right\} \qquad (9)$$

Further statistical analysis of (7) reveals interesting mobility prediction models that can be derived from this relation. As an illustration, if the memory level parameter α is now zero, then Gauss-Markov Model becomes memory-less as depicted in (10):

$$v_t^x = v^x + \sigma^x w_{t-1}^x$$
$$v_t^y = v^y + \sigma^y w_{t-1}^y$$
$$\left.\begin{array}{l}\end{array}\right\} \qquad (10)$$

In this scenario, the velocity of mobile station at timeslot t is only determined by the fixed drift velocity given by (11) and the Gaussian random variable given by (12):

$$\bar{v} = [v^x, v^y]^T \qquad (11)$$
$$\overline{W}_{t-1} = [w_{t-1}^x, w_{t-1}^y] \qquad (12)$$

The mobility model depicted in (10) is the random walk model. On the other hand, if the memory level α is one, relation (9) becomes:

$$v_t^x = v_{t-1}^x$$
$$v_t^y = v_{t-1}^y$$
$$\left.\begin{array}{l}\end{array}\right\} \qquad (13)$$

where the velocity of mobile station at time slot t is exactly same as its previous velocity. The model depicted this way is the fluid flow model.

In as much as deterministic models are able to characterize pretty fairly the first order or second order kinetic models with constant accelerations, a velocity subject to an unknown acceleration or known but non-constant acceleration requires the use of more complex stochastic models. In addition, the prediction of the location of a mobile station using the Gauss-Markov as a function of time requires that the last reported location and velocity be established in advance.

4.4 Cell to Cell Mobility Models

These models are history based in that they are utilized to predict the mobile stations macro-mobility, or the cell to cell mobility. Here, a repetition of routine movements permits the easy discovery of the mobile station' favorite paths.

One technique to describe mobile station mobility regularities is to record a set of User Mobility Patterns (UMP) stored in a profile for each user and indexed by the incident time. Examples of these models include the *global mobility prediction model, neuro-fuzzy inference model*, and the *shadow cluster model.*

The major complexity in these models is to evaluate the sensitivity between the UMP and the User Actual Path (UAP). As an illustration, is a UAP which diverges from the UMP by a single cell a small variation of the same path, or a totally new path not reported in the profile? Approximate Pattern-matching techniques can be employed to discover the UMP that fits best to a UAP.

Suppose that a UMP is described by a cell sequence given in (14):

$$(a_1 a_2 \dots a_{i-1} a_i a_{i+1} \dots a_n) \tag{14}$$

Then the expected movement of a mobile station can be modeled as an edited UMP by permitting the following legal options:

Introducing a cell c at position i of the UMP yields UAP shown in (15):

$$(a_1 a_2, \dots a_{i-1} c a_i a_{i+1} \dots a_n) \tag{15}$$

Erasing cell a_i at position i of the UMP results in UAP shown in (16):

$$(a_1 a_2, \dots a_{i-1} a_{i+1} \dots a_n) \tag{16}$$

Shifting cell a_i to another cell c provides UAP shown in (17):

$$(a_1 a_2, \dots a_{i-1} c a_{i+1} \dots a_n) \tag{17}$$

In this approach, the degree of resemblance of a UAP with a UMP is determined by computing the edit distance, which is a finite string comparison metric. This is normally accomplished by establishing the smallest number of insertion, erasure and modifications by which two cell sequences can be made identical. As such, if the edit distance is less than a matching threshold t, an approximately matched UMP is established, signifying the common moving objective of the user and the macro-prediction may be done accordingly.

In essence, the mobile station's inter-cell directional movement intention is approximated by representing UAP as an edited version of a UMP and using an estimate pattern-matching procedure to discern the UMP that most bear a resemblance to UAP.

4.5 Models Based On Feasible Future Sequence of Cells

In these mobility models, the sequence of cells a user is likely to utilize in the future is treated as a criterion for mobile station mobility prediction. These models are hierarchic in nature in that they include a micro-prediction algorithm coupled with a macro-prediction schema. As such, stochastic models are employed for micro-prediction, while history-based models are utilized for macro-prediction. The strengths of these models are that they are capable of predicting with a very high precision the sequence of cells users will employ in the future. In addition, they can compute the time the user will reach the boundary of each cell. Examples of these models are *hierarchical models*.

In these models, user mobility prediction is accomplished in two levels: local prediction (LP) and global prediction (GP). Whereas GP identifies the overall movement pattern of a mobile station and predicts mobility only at the macroscopic level, LP achieves a high degree of accuracy for next-cell prediction devoid of any postulation of the mobile station mobility history. In so doing, the UMP identification error is significantly reduced since GP employs the prediction data from LP to look ahead before making a decision on the best matched pattern.

Local prediction is achieved using a two-step process: assessment of the dynamic state of a mobile station utilizing subsequent received signal strength indicator measurements; and the selection of the neighboring cell with maximum cell-crossing probability as LP output based on dynamic state estimation and cell geometry.

Neighboring cell selection is carried out when the mobile station moves in an area that is closer to the cell boundary, and where the chances of it making a spectacular change in its direction and speed are negligible. This area is referred to as the correlation area of the neighboring cell i, denoted as Γ_i, for i = 1, ..., 6 in a hexagonal cell structure, where:

$$\Gamma_i = \{X_n | [x(n), y(n)] \in \beta_i, d_0 \geq d_t \text{ and } \theta \in [\theta_i, \theta_{i+1}]\} \tag{18}$$

In this regard, β_i is the 60° sector adjacent to neighboring cell i, d_0 is the distance between mobile station with coordinates $[x(n), y(n)]$ and the serving base transceiver station with coordinates (a_0, b_0), d_t is the distance threshold that determines the confidence in the prediction results, θ is the direction of motion, and θ_i is the bearing of cell vertex V_i, $i = 1, \dots.6$. Mobile stations with high velocities have been observed to be prone in following straight line constant velocity trajectories compared to those with lower velocities. As such, d_t can be set dynamically to realize early prediction for a given prediction confidence. Upon entry into the correlated area, the mobile station cell-crossing probability can be computed based on its dynamic state as follows:

$$P_r(cell_i/X_n) = \int_{\theta_i}^{\theta_{i+1}} f(\theta/X_n)d_\theta, \text{ with } i = 1, \dots 6 \tag{19}$$

where $f(\theta/X_n)$ is the probability density function of the direction of motion θ given the dynamic state X_n. Applying the minimum error prediction criterion, the prediction result of the next crossing cell becomes:

$$Next_{Cell}/X_n = \arg \max_i\{P_r(cell_i/X_n)\}, \ i = 1, \dots 6 \tag{20}$$

Unfortunately, the computation of $P_r(cell_i/X_n)$ is quite involving because θ is non-linearly related to the dynamic state, X_n.

4.6 Models Based On Degree Of Randomness

The mobility prediction models that are based on degree of randomness fall into three categories: *trace based, constrained topology* and *statistical* models. Trace based models include *deterministic models* while constrained topology models consist of *city section mobility*, the *street unit model*, *mobility vector, obstacle mobility*, and *city area mobility* models. On their part, statistical models include *random walk, random waypoint, Markovian Random Walk, smooth random mobility, random direction, shortest path*, and *normal walk* models.

4.6.1 Trace-Based Models

In trace based models, everything is deterministic since mobile station' movement is mapped out in their real life scenarios. For instance, a deterministic process such as mobile station velocity $V(t)$ at a particular time t can be described as follows:

$$V(t) = V cos(\omega_0 t + \tau) \tag{21}$$

where V, ω_0 and τ are all non-random variables. It is also possible for one or all of these variables to be arbitrary, in which case this velocity becomes deterministic random process. The consequence of this is that any one sample function corresponds to (21) with particular values of these random variables. As such, knowledge of the sample function prior to any time instant automatically permits the prediction of the sample function's future values, such as the mobile station velocity since its form is known. The variation of the components of the mobile station velocity such as amplitude, angular frequency, or phase may create a wide range of mobility models that may also fall into the category of the deterministic mobility model.

4.6.2 Constrained Topology Models

Constrained topology models provide some partial randomness, which simulate real life scenarios where mobile station movement is controlled by obstacles or pathways; but speed and direction are still randomly chosen.

A. Mobility Vector Models

In these models, the velocity of any mobile station is composed of a primary velocity component and a deviation from this vector:

$$\vec{M} = \vec{B} + \alpha \vec{V} \tag{22}$$

In this case, $\vec{M}$ is the mobility vector, $\vec{B}$ is the base vector, α is the acceleration and $\vec{V}$ is the deviation vector. The deviation vector is significant in making movement smooth and permits the design of more realistic scenarios. This is due to the possibility of mimicking the deceleration of a mobile station approaching its destination or the acceleration of a mobile station at the beginning of the movement process. The base vector represents the primary velocity component of a single mobile station and the deviation vector characterizes the divergence from the base vector. Numerous mobility patterns can be produced by changing vector $\vec{B}$, $\vec{V}$ and α, such as the *Reference Point Group Mobility* Model. Effectively, this model allows the description of a large set of scenarios since it can be applied to other models, such as the Random Waypoint model so that the results will be more realistic.

B. Obstacle Mobility Model

To represent the prospective pathways that exist in the presence of obstacles, Voronoi diagrams are employed. These Voronoi-based pathways generalize the insightful perception that the pathways naturally run in the middle of two adjacent buildings. The classical concept of Voronoi diagrams from computational geometry can be investigated by considering a set of n points in the 2D plane:

$$P = \{p_1, p_2, \ldots p_n\} \tag{23}$$

Each of these points is regarded as a location point. The Voronoi diagram of P is a partition of the plane into convex polygonal cells, one cell per location point, so that every point in a cell is closer to its location point than to any other location point. As such, a Voronoi cell of a location point p_i can be thought of as p_i's region of influence. The boundary edges of the cells are straight line segments, and each segment is equidistant from its two closest location points.

4.6.3 Statistical Models

In these models, mobile stations shift to any destination and their velocities and directions are selected randomly. The motion pattern of individual mobile stations is described by some stochastic process.

A. Random Walk Model

This is an individual mobility model. A one dimensional random walk can be considered a Markov chain whose state space is given by integers:

$$i = \pm 1, \pm 2, \ldots \quad \text{for some number } 0 < p < 1, \pi_{i,i+1} = p = \pi_{i,i-1} \tag{24}$$

where $\pi_{k,l}$ represents the probability of transition from state k to l. This model is called random walk since it may be thought as being a representation for an individual walking on a straight line, who at each point in time takes either one step to the right with probability p or one step to the left with probability $1 - p$. The implication is that random walk is a simple stochastic process. Here, a mobile station changes its speed and direction for each time interval, and has zero pause time. The velocity $v(t)$ is selected from the predefined ranges $[V_{min}, V_{max}]$ by each mobile station following a uniform distribution or Gaussian distribution at every new interval t. In this case, V_{min} and V_{max} are the

30

minimum velocity and the maximum velocity respectively. In addition, each mobile station picks its new direction $\theta(t)$ arbitrarily and uniformly from the ranges $[0, 2\pi]$. For each time interval t, a mobile station moves with a velocity vector given by:

$$v(t)\cos\theta, v(t)\sin\theta \qquad (25)$$

B. Random Waypoint Model

Taking $P_i^{(J)}$ as a vector spelling out that the mobile station picks its movement interval i, the movement trace of a mobile station j can be described as a discrete-time stochastic process, given by selecting a random waypoint $P_i^{(J)}$ for each movement period i:

$$\{P_i^{(J)}\}_{i \in N} = P_0^{(J)}, P_1^{(J)}, P_2^{(J)}, P_3^{(J)}, \ldots \qquad (26)$$

To depict the movement process of a mobile station within the coverage area, the postulation that the waypoints are independently and identically distributed (IID) over the coverage area A with a uniform random distribution is taken. In addition, the index j is omitted since each mobile station moves independently of other mobile stations and hence the study of the stochastic process of a single mobile station is satisfactory. Suppose that a mobile station picks a new speed V_i for movement from P_{i-1} to P_i and a pause time $T_{p,i}$ at waypoint P_i arbitrarily. Then the movement process is depicted as follows:

$$\left.\begin{aligned} \{(P_i, V_i, T_{p,i})\}_{i \in N} &= (P_1, V_1, T_{p,1}), \\ (P_2, V_1, T_{p,2}), \\ (P_3, V_3, T_{p,3}), \ldots \end{aligned}\right\} \qquad (27)$$

Here, an additional waypoint P_0 is necessary for initialization and $\{(p_i, v_i, \tau_{p,i})\}_{i \in N}$ is utilized to express a sample of this process. The vector $(p_{i-1}, p_i, v_i, \tau_{p,i})$ characterizes the movement period i entirely. The probability density function (PDF) of the pause time, $T_{p,i}$ is described by $fT_p(\tau_p)$ in the interval $(0, \tau_{p,max})$ with $\tau_{p,max} < \infty$ and the probable value of the pause time is a definite function depicted by $E(T_p)$. Here, the values of the pause time are selected from these random functions. On the same breadth, $fT_p(\tau_p)$ is the PDF of the velocity bounded by the interval $[v_{min}, v_{max}]$ with $v_{min} > 0$ and $v_{max}, < \infty$ and the values of the velocity are picked from this PDF.

C. Markovian Random Walk

In this model, each entry of the transition matrix $P(i, j)$ is employed to indicate the probability that a mobile station will shift from state i to state j. Considering a three state system, $P(i, j)$ can be represented as follows:

$$P(i,j) = \begin{bmatrix} P(0,0) & P(0,1) & P(0,2) \\ P(1,0) & P(1,1) & P(1,2) \\ P(2,0) & P(2,1) & P(2,2) \end{bmatrix} \tag{28}$$

The values within this transition probability matrix are utilized to revise the mobile station's x and y locations. As an illustration, Figure 1 shows the particular Markov chain for the three states (0, 1, & 2) with probability for each movement specified on the arcs.

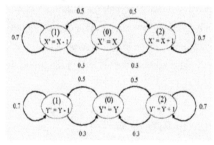

Figure 1: Markov Chain and Probability Matrix

In this figure, X and Y represents the current x and y coordinates respectively while X' and Y' denote subsequent x and y coordinates respectively. Using the probabilities in this diagram, transition matrix P_1 can be constructed as follows:

$$P_1 = \begin{bmatrix} 0.0 & 0.5 & 0.5 \\ 0.3 & 0.7 & 0.0 \\ 0.3 & 0.0 & 0.7 \end{bmatrix} \tag{29}$$

Upon the definition of the state transition probabilities in form of matrix, a mobile station may take a step in any of the four probable directions towards north, south, east, or west as long as it continues to move with no pause time. However, the values in the state transition matrix prohibit movements between the previous and the next positions without passing through the current location.

D. Random Direction Model

Considering a walk segment with index i starting at point $X_i = (x_i, y_1)$, with an absolute angle φ_i, unit vector along the absolute angle $a(\varphi_i)$, the length l_i , the velocity v_i, and the pause time at the beginning of the walk segment $t_{p,i}$, the subsequent waypoint X_{i+1} for the next time interval t_{i+1} is given as follows:

$$\left. \begin{aligned} X_{i+1} &= X_i + a(\varphi_i).l_i \\ t_{i+1} &= t_i + t_{p,i} + i_i/v_i \end{aligned} \right\} \tag{30}$$

The mobile station employing this model treats the parameters for a walk segment as arbitrary variables with following uniform distributions:

$$\left. \begin{aligned} \varphi_i &= \Phi & &: \text{Uniform } [0, 2\pi] \\ l_i &= L & &: \text{Uniform } [L_{min}, L_{max}] \\ v_i &= V & &: \text{Uniform } [V_{min}, V_{max}] \\ t_{p,i} &= T_p & &: \text{Uniform } [T_{p,min}, T_{p,max}] \end{aligned} \right\} \tag{31}$$

As such, the parameterization is reduced to the choice of the constructs, $L_{min}, L_{max}, V_{min}, V_{max}, T_{p,min}$ and $T_{p,max}$. The greatest challenge of this model is the requirement that that a border behavior model be specified for the reaction of mobile stations reaching the simulation area boundary.

E. Shortest Path Model

The graph employed here has vertices or nodes denoted by v or u. The weighted edges that connect two nodes (u, v) symbolize an edge while $w (u, v)$ designate its weight. To employ this model, three constructs are initialized: $dist, Q$ and S. In this case, $dist$ is an array of distances from the source node to each node in the graph, instantiated as follows:

$$dist(s) = 0 \ and$$
$$dist(s) = \infty \ for \ all \ other \ nodes, v \qquad \left.\right\} \qquad (32)$$

This is carried out at the beginning of the search process, and as the algorithm proceeds, the $dist$ from the source to each node v in the graph will be recalculated and finalized when the shortest distance to the destination is determined. On the other hand, Q is a queue of all nodes in the graph, implying that at the end of the algorithm's execution, Q will be empty. On its part, S is an empty set which serves to indicate the nodes the algorithm has already visited. Consequently, on completion of the search process, S will contain all the nodes of the graph. The procedure of determining the shortest path proceeds as follows: While Q is not empty, the model picks from Q the node with the smallest $dist(v)$ that is not already in S.

In the first run, source node s will be selected since $dist(s)$ is initialized to 0. In the next run, the next node with the smallest $dist$ value is selected. Thereafter, node v is added to S to indicate that v has now been visited. This is followed by an update of $dist$ values of adjacent nodes of the current node v. This updating is accomplished as follows: for each new adjacent node u, given that $dist(v) + wight(u, v) < dist(u)$, there is a new minimal distance found for u. As such, $dist(u)$ is updated to the new minimal distance value. However, if $dist(v) + wight(u, v) > dist(u)$, no updates are made to $dist(u)$. At the end of the search process, the algorithm would have visited all nodes in the graph and found the smallest distance to each node. Therefore, $dist$ now contains the shortest path from source to the destination.

F. Normal Walk Models
In this model, the ith move, Y_i, is arrived at by rotating the $(i-1)^{th}$ move, Y_{i-1}, counterclockwise for θ_i degrees as follows:

$$Y_i = R(\theta_i)Y_{i-1} \qquad (33)$$

where θ_i is normally distributed with zero mean. Due to the fact that this model selects the normal distribution with zero mean, the probability density increases as the rotation angle approaches zero. As such, a mobile station has a very high probability of preserving its previous movement direction.

34

G. Smooth Random Mobility Model

In this model, the rate of velocity change follows a Poisson process. When velocity change happens, a new target velocity $v(t)$ is picked and then the velocity of mobile station is adjusted incrementally from the current velocity $v(t')$ to the targeted new velocity $v(t)$ by acceleration velocity or deceleration velocity, $a(t)$. The probability distribution function of acceleration or deceleration $a(t)$ is homogeneously distributed among $[0, a_{max}]$ and $[a_{min}, 0]$ respectively. For each time slot t, the new velocity is calculated as follows:

$$v(t) = v(t - \Delta t) + a(t)\Delta t \tag{34}$$

Consequently, the mobile station velocity may be controlled to increase or decrease continuously and incrementally. If $a(t)$ is a small value, velocity is altered gradually and the level of temporal correlation is strong. However, if $a(t)$ is big enough, velocity can be adjusted swiftly and the temporal correlation is small. The direction change consists of several time steps until the new direction is achieved. This produces a smooth curve rather than a sharp turning. Unlike velocity, the movement direction is postulated to be entirely evenly spread in the interval $[0, 2\pi]$ .Each mobile station has an initial direction $\varphi(t = 0)$ which is selected from a uniform distribution:

$$f_\Phi(\varphi) = \frac{1}{2\pi}, 0 \le \varphi \le 2\pi, \varphi \in \Phi \tag{35}$$

A mobile station moves in a straight line until a direction change occurs, which is influenced by a stochastic process. This happens with a probability $f_\Phi(\varphi) << 1$ each time step. For the case of continuous time motion, the time between two direction changes follows an exponential distribution with a mean time between two direction changes of:

$$\mu_\varphi * = \frac{\Delta t}{f_\Phi(\varphi*)} = \frac{1}{f_\Phi(\varphi)} s \tag{36}$$

In situations where a mobile station is anticipated to change its direction, a new target direction φ^* is chosen from equation (35).

4.7 Models Based On Level of Description

Mobility models employing levels of description fall into three categories: *microscopic, mesoscopic,* and *macroscopic* models. In these models, the number of mobile stations is considered as being key in the mobility prediction process. Microscopic models include *Street Unit Models* and *Street Pattern Tracing* models while Mesoscopic models include *Reference Point Group Mobility* (In-Place Mobility, Overlap Mobility, and Convention Mobility) and *Mobility Vector* model. On their part, macroscopic models comprise of *fluid flow* models, *gravity* models and the *random walk* models.

4.7.1 Fluid Flow Model

In this model, it is postulated that a mobile station moves in direction uniformly distributed over (0, 2π). This model considers the amount of traffic flow out of a region to be proportional to the mobile station density within the region, the average velocity, and the length of the region boundary. Taking into consideration a circular region with a mobile station density of ρ, an average velocity $\bar{v}$, and region diameter of D, the average number of cell crossings per unit time N_{avg} is computed as follows:

$$N_{avg} = \rho \pi D \bar{v} \tag{37}$$

This model has been utilized in association with the communications network traffic volume which is also a function of mobile station velocities. In this scenario, it expresses a relationship between three parameters: mobile station average velocity $\bar{v}$ with direction uniformly distributed over $(0, 2\pi)$, mobile station density (ρ), and mobile station volume of communications networking traffic (q). In such cases, it is referred to as the fluid-flow traffic model and is expressed follows:

$$q = \rho \bar{v} \tag{38}$$

Equation (38) implies that when the density of vehicles on a road goes up, speed goes down and vice versa.

4.7.2 Gravity Mobility Models

Here, the number of mobile stations present at a specific location is dependent on the attractivity of the location, which can be formulated as follows:

$$F_{ij} = G \frac{P_i P_j}{d_{ij}} \tag{39}$$

In this case, F_{ij} is the matrix element representing the force of attractivity of a mobile station shifting from location i to location j; P_i and P_j are importance of the location of origin location i and the location of destination j, respectively; d_{ij} is the distance between the location of origin and the location of destination. This can be considered as a kind of resistance factor that forces a mobile station to transit from location i to location j; and G is proportionality constant related to the rate of the event. For instance, considering the same system of spatial interactions, the value of G will be higher when interactions are observed for a month compared to the value of G for one day. In a nutshell, the gravity mobility model expresses the mobility parameters in terms of the spatial interactions between locations i and j which are proportional to their respective importance divided by their distance of separation.

4.8 Models Based On Individual User Behaviors

These models represent the specific motion of mobile stations at small scales levels. They decompose mobility into simple atomic individual behaviors and the combination of these behaviors yields practical displacement patterns. This is achieved by reproducing the mobility observed at small scales in everyday life, in both space and time. The models in this grouping include *activity-based* and *cell-residence-time-based* models.

Considering $R_i(\tau)$ to be the residence time before a mobile station shifts out of the cell, then for cell-residence time based models, when a mobile station arrives at cell i in timeslot Δ_τ, the expected value $E[R_i(\tau)]$ can be derived by Little's Law:

$$N = \lambda R \tag{40}$$

where N is the anticipated number of mobile station in a cell , λ is the arrival rate of the mobile stations , and R is the probable response time that a mobile station stays in the cell. Considering cell i in timeslot Δ_τ, Little's Law can be re-written as follows:

$$E[N_i(\tau)] = \lambda_i(\tau) E[R_i(\tau)] \tag{41}$$

In this case, $E[N_i(\tau)]$ is the expected number of mobile stations in cell i. The expected cell residence time, $E[R_i(\tau)]$ can be computed by taking into consideration the number of calls arriving at cell i in Δ_τ and the number of handovers into cell i in timeslot Δ_τ:

$$E[R_i(\tau)] = \frac{\rho_i(\tau)}{\gamma_i(\tau)} \qquad (42)$$

where $\rho_i(\tau)$ the number of calls arriving at cell i in Δ_τ, which can also be regarded as the minutes of traffic of cell i in Δ_τ. On the other hand, $\gamma_i(\tau)$ is the the number of handovers into cell i in timeslot Δ_τ.

4.9 Models Based On Nodes Movement Dependency

In this taxonomy, a mobile station movement may be influenced by that of other mobile stations within the network coverage area. This dependency can be in form of temporal dependency of velocity or spatial dependency of velocity.

4.9.1 Temporal Dependency of Velocity

Models with this feature take into consideration the fact that in many real life scenarios, the speed of vehicles and pedestrians accelerates incrementally. In addition, the motion direction change occurs smoothly rather than suddenly. Examples of these models include *Gauss-Markov mobility,* and *smooth random mobility.* This is in sharp contrast to random walk models such as the random waypoint model where the velocity of mobile station is a memory-less random process, meaning that the velocity at the current epoch is independent of that of the previous epoch. Consequently, some severe mobility behavior such as abrupt stop, sudden acceleration and sharp turn, may transpire in the trace generated by random walk models.

4.9.2 Spatial Dependency of Velocity

Models with this characteristic appreciate the fact that in some scenarios such as battlefield communication and museum touring, the movement pattern of a mobile station may be influenced by certain specific leader mobile station in its vicinity. Consequently, the mobility of various mobile stations can be correlated. Examples of these models include *reference point group mobility, column mobility, pursue mobility*, and *nomadic community mobility.* This contrasts random walk models such as random waypoint that consider the mobile station as an entity that moves independently of other mobile nodes.

A. Reference Point Group Mobility

Here, the motion of a group leader at time t is described by a motion vector $\vec{V}^t{}_{group}$. Since this model depicts both group leader and group members' movement patterns, each member of this group deviates from this common motion vector by some degree. Effectively, the movement of group members is considerably influenced by the movement of its group leader. Specifically, the motion vector of group member i at time t , $\vec{V}^t{}_i$ is formulated as follows:

$$\vec{V}^t{}_i = \vec{V}^t{}_{group} + \bar{R}\vec{M}^t{}_i \tag{43}$$

For each mobile station, mobility is assigned a reference point that tracks the group movement. In this case, the motion vector $\bar{R}\vec{M}^t{}_i$ is an arbitrary vector deviated by group member i from its own reference point. The vector $\bar{R}\vec{M}^t{}_i$ is an independent identically distributed (IID) random process whose length is uniformly distributed in the interval $[0, r_{max}]$ and whose direction is uniformly distributed in the interval $[0, 2\pi]$. In this model, r_{max} is the maximum allowed distance deviation.

B. Column Mobility Model

In this model, at time slot t, the mobile station i updates its reference point RP_i^t by adding an advance vector α_i^t to its previous reference point RP_i^{t-1}. Statistically, this new reference point is represented as follows:

$$RP_i^t = RP_i^{t-1} + \alpha_i^t \tag{44}$$

The advance vector α_i^t is the predefined offset utilized to shift the reference grid of mobile station i at time t. After the reference point has been revised, the new position of mobile station i randomly deviates from the revised reference point by a random vector w_i^t . Specifically:

$$P_i^t = RP_i^t + w_i^t \tag{45}$$

Pursue Mobility Model

The mobile stations acting as seekers in this model direct their velocity towards the position of the targeted mobile station and attempt to intercept it. Mathematically, this can be expressed as:

$$P_i^t = P_i^{t-1} + v_i^t \left(P_{target}^t - P_i^{t-1} \right) + w_i^t \tag{46}$$

In this case, P^t_{target} is the projected position of the targeted mobile station being pursued at time t and w^t_i is a small random vector utilized to offset the movement of mobile station i.

C. Nomadic Community Mobility Model

In this model, the entire group of mobile stations moves randomly from one location to another and the reference point of each mobile station is established based on the common movement of the entire group. Inside this group, each mobile station has the capability of offsetting some random vector to its predefined reference point:

$$P^t_i = RP^t_i + w^t_i \tag{47}$$

In this case, w^t_i is a small random vector employed to offset the movement of mobile station i at time t. When compared with column mobility model which also depends on the reference grid, it is observed that mobile stations in the nomadic community mobility model share the same reference grid while in column mobility model, each mobile station has its own reference point. In addition, the movement in the nomadic community model is intermittent while the movement is more or less constant in column mobility model.

4.10 Models Based On Real Network Movement Depiction

In this taxonomical unit, three categories of mobility models were identified as *realistic, unrealistic* and *geographically restricted mobility* models. The realistic models include column mobility models such as *pursue mobility, nomadic community mobility, reference point group mobility* (in-place mobility, overlap mobility, convention mobility). On their part, unrealistic models include *random way point mobility* (random walk mobility, random direction mobility), *Gauss-Markov mobility*, and *Manhattan grid mobility*. The geographically restricted models consist of *pathway mobility, obstacle mobility, Freeway mobility*, and *Manhattan mobility*. The statistical of these models have already been elaborated above.

PART V

CRITIC OF GSM MOBILITY PREDICTION MODELS

5.1 Introduction

Having mathematically analyzed the various GSM mobility prediction models, a number of flaws were easily identified in these models that present some operational challenges when these models are applied in a real GSM mobile station mobility prediction environment. The discussion on these drawbacks is elaborated using the nine taxonomical categories that were developed.

5.2 Models Based On Location and Fixed Velocity

It was observed that both Feynman-Verlet and first order kinetic model employ a constant velocity. Therefore these models cannot be employed to predict the actual movement of mobile stations within the GSM coverage area, where the velocities of mobile users change frequently. In addition, when varying velocity is used for these models, position predictions are computed using a velocity one step ahead. Consequently, these models require two samples of past velocities and two piecewise constant accelerations to be known in order to predict the future mobile station position.

In Manhattan model, the map of the network coverage area must be employed and a mobile station is permitted to transit only along the grid of horizontal and vertical streets on the map. This makes it ideal in modeling movement in urban areas where a persistent computing service between portable devices is offered. However, it cannot be employed in rural areas where no streets or highways exist. In addition, this model requires a very detailed analysis of the mobile station motion, highway and street type under any vehicular traffic conditions.

Freeway mobility model on the other hand utilizes a random graph to represent the map of a city. Here, the vertices of the graph symbolize the buildings of the city, and the edges depict the streets and freeways between these buildings. At the start of the simulation, the mobile stations are placed randomly on the edges of the graph. Then for each mobile station, a destination is randomly selected and the mobile station moves towards this destination through the shortest path along the edges. Upon arrival, the mobile station pauses for T_p time and again picks a new destination for the subsequent movement. This procedure is repeated until the end of simulation. As was the case for Manhattan model, the mobility is restricted to the pathways in the map.

5.3 Models Based On High Probability Prediction

Mobility predictions using these models require that the last reported location and the previous velocity, V_{t-1}, of the mobile station be known in advance. In these schemes, a mobile station's future location is predicted by the network, using the information gathered from the mobile's recent report of location and velocity. When a call is made, the GSM network pages the destination mobile station around the envisaged location. A mobile station performs the same location prediction as the network does by inspecting its own location periodically and reporting the new location when the distance between the predicted and the actual locations exceeds a given threshold. As a result, a total of three parameters, previous location, previous velocity and the threshold distance must be known before prediction can be accomplished.

5.4 Cell to Cell Mobility Models

The cell to cell mobility models such as global mobility models have a number of drawbacks that make them inefficient in real network aplications. To begin with, these models require a set of mobility patterns to be stored in a profile for each user. This introduces some space complexity on the side of the network infrastructure. Secondly, there are complexities in assessing the sensitivity between user mobility patterns and the user actual path. In addition, these models are concerned with macro-movements, hence not suited for individual user movements.

5.5 Models Based On Feasible Future Sequence of Cells

In hierarchical mobility prediction models, both LP and GP measurements must be carried out. Since these two parameters require regular measurements, this leads to high signaling traffic in the network. In addition, these quantities need updating for every cycle; and doing so at higher rates result in a substantial amount of computational costs. To reduce signaling traffic, buffering of the historical long-term movement patterns (UMPs) and the current movement history (UAP) within the mobile station is required in order to guarantee security against unwanted predictors and locators. However, this introduces space complexity at the mobile station. Moreover, these models require additional information such as cell identification numbers and cell topology to operate correctly. Since this

42

information can only be obtained from the base station broadcasting on a protected control channel at the beacon frequency in each cell, this adds to the problem of high signaling traffic.

5.6 Models Based On Degree of Randomness

In trace based models, the main challenges are that are that since GSM is a fairly new research area, no real operational system is available yet to provide the required real life traces for mobile users. In addition, it is a very complicated task to accurately trace the mobility pattern of the users within the network coverage areas. Despite the fact that analytical models have been developed for the evaluation of the effects of fixed channel allocation scheme, user load, mobility and distribution of users among cells on system performance, these models presume a fixed population of users moving in a finite set of cells, and hence they do not depict a real life scenario.

Considering obstacle mobility models, the common scenarios represented are city centers or campuses. Here, a mobile station randomly selects a building as its destination, shifts towards it, then pauses there for a while and finally transits to another building. The mobile station moves to its destination by picking the shortest path to the destination. Unfortunately, to reach a destination, the mobile station can only move along pathways. In addition, this model takes another assumption that is not realistic, that the communication of a mobile station with other mobile stations will be totally blocked by buildings if the transmission is out of line of sight.

However, for the case of street unit model, the Manhattan grid is utilized to represent many square grid cities. Here, employing dummy streets, irregular paths can be designated to the desired approximation degree. However, this increases the computation effort and complexity of path computations.

For the case of street area mobility model, the means to estimate the query load of a distributed database that spans the entire city area can be offered, in addition to useful results for paging area dimensioning and location area planning schemes. However, the assumptions about population distribution are not applicable for long time periods. Instead, since mobility conditions in a city area are fairly dynamic, this population distribution remains true only for short periods.

In statistical models, the mobile station is assumed to have the capability of moving in any direction. However, this is not realistic, since mobile users are not able to move anywhere and in real world scenarios, users cannot move randomly without any destination in mind. Physical obstacles such as buildings can deter users from moving randomly within the network coverage areas. Another challenge is that in the random walk mobility model, when the specified time and the distance that a mobile station shifts are short, then the roaming pattern is limited to a small portion of the network coverage area. In addition, these modes suffer from limitations such as lack of temporal dependency of velocity, lack of spatial dependency of velocity and failure to recognize geographic restrictions on movement, and restrictions in pause time. In temporal dependency of velocity, the moving direction of a mobile station at time $t + 1$ is selected randomly from a uniform distribution process ranging from 0 to $360°$. Due to their memory-less nature, this direction is independent of its previous direction at time t. As such, in these models, there may be situations where the motion style of a mobile station follows an oscillatory-type trajectory, moving forward and backward, yielding an impractical mobility model. In spatial dependency of velocity, random walk models regard the mobile station as an entity moving independently of other mobile stations. However, in some real world scenarios such as battlefield communication, the movement pattern of a mobile station may be influenced by another mobile station acting as a leader in its neighborhood. In this situation, the mobility of various mobile stations is correlated, implying that random walk models may not correctly reflect the group mobile stations behavior. For the case of geographic restrictions of movement, these models assume that the mobile stations move freely within the coverage areas without any precincts. However, in realistic cases such as those ones involving urban areas, the movement of a mobile station may be bounded by obstacles, buildings, streets, or freeways. Moreover, these models consider the mobile station as moving without any pause time, which is idealistic.

With regard to random waypoint model, a mobile station randomly picks a destination, called waypoint, in the network coverage area and then moves towards it on a straight line with constant velocity. This velocity is randomly selected from a given range, $[V_{min}, V_{max}]$ uniformly distributed. Then it pauses for a while before it again picks a new destination. On reaching the destination, the station pauses for some time distributed according to some arbitrary variable and the process repeats itself. Once the pause time expires, the mobile station selects a new destination, speed, and pause time. Since it is based on random selection of destinations, pause times and velocity, it inherits all the setbacks of random walk models.

Considering the Markov model, it was noted that the movements in the horizontal and vertical directions as well as stops are not possible for interval of time greater than one step. Additionally, once a mobile station has commenced movement, it is likely to remain in the same direction. This is because the probability that it stays in states (1) or (2) of the Markov chain is greater than the probability that it goes back to state (0). Moreover, this model does not permit abrupt changes to the way the mobile station is moving since there is no one-step transition between states (1) and (2). The implication is that the mobile station has to stop before changing the direction of motion. In the shortest path model, a mobile station can only go straight or make a left or right turn at an intersection. In addition, a mobile station cannot make two consecutive left turns or right turns.

For normal walk models, a mobile station has a very high probability of retaining its previous movement direction.

5.7 Models Based On Level of Description

Microscopic model are concerned with the movement of a single mobile station, hence not ideal for depicting the movement of a group of users. Mesoscopic models depict the homogenized movement behaviour of several mobile stations instead of only one, hence not suitable for describing mobility pattern of a single user. On their part, macroscopic models confine themselves to density, mean speed, speed variance, and traffic flow of vehicles. Specifically, the fluid flow model is only suited for representing traffic on highways and is inadequate for describing individual movements including stopping and starting. This model does not satisfactorily reflect correlation between density and speed. In addition, it requires a constant movement with infrequent speed and direction changes. Moreover, this model is deficient for individual mobile station movements with stop-and-go interruption. Here, the average density and average velocity of the mobile stations of the entire population are utilized and as such, the model is more accurate for regions with high populations.

5.8 Models Based On Individual User Behaviors

In activity based models, the location for the next activity has to be established first before a route from the current location to this activity location can be calculated in terms of cells crossed. In cell-residence-time-based model, there is a requirement for the tracing of the movement of individual users. The measurement of cell residence times in a commercially operated mobile network is a very complicated task due to its dynamic nature.

5.9 Models Based On Nodes Movement Dependency

These models are good at depicting movements with temporal dependency of velocity and spatial dependency of velocity. Therefore, they cannot be used to describe movement patterns for mobile stations moving as an atomic entity within the GSM network coverage area. Additionally, to derive the velocity of group member, two constructs, the group velocity and the motion vector, which is a random vector deviated by group member from its own reference point, must be known beforehand.

5.10 Models Based On Real Network Movement Depiction

Some models such as pursue mobility, nomadic community mobility, and reference point group mobility are suited for depicting motion for a group of mobile stations but not individual subscribers. In addition, obstacle mobility makes an unrealistic assumption that the mobile station signal is completely absorbed by the obstacle on its path. On their part, pathway mobility, Freeway mobility, and Manhattan mobility restrict movements to the streets on the maps, hence not ideal for realistic movements that involve streets and pedestrian pathways not indicated on the map.

PART VI

PROPOSED MOBILITY PREDICTION MODEL

6.1 Introduction

Numerous flaws have been noted in the current mobile station mobility prediction models. As such, there is need for an inclusive mobility prediction model that takes some realistic assumptions.

6.2 Requirements for the Proposed Model

Since majority of mobile users move individually within the network coverage area, the first necessity is that the mobility prediction should be based on atomic movements. Even within groups, each user moves with an atomic reference point and are allowed to deviate from the group velocity by some random vector. The second requirement is that the proposed mobility prediction model should be stochastic since users within the GSM network coverage area are able to move in any direction. However, the proposed mobility model should recognize real life scenarios such as obstacles and hence the third prerequisite is that the movement should be pseudo-stochastic.

The current obstacle mobility model assumes that the mobile station signal is completely absorbed by the obstacle, which is impractical. As such, the fourth condition is that the proposed mobility model should assume that only movement is blocked by the obstacle and the signals can still reach their intended destination without being blocked by the obstacle. This is because the communication between the BTS and the mobile station uses radio waves that can travel even within openings within an obstacle such as pavements within buildings. The fifth obligation is that the obstacle should force the mobile station to bounce off and look for alternative paths to the destination. Since the current mobility prediction models do not take care of base transceiver stations overlapping regions, the sixth requirement is that the proposed mobility prediction model should be able to depict movement patterns within these locations.

Conclusions

The aim of this paper was to carry out a statistical analysis of the current mobility prediction models so as to understand how they fail when applied in actual GSM mobile station mobility prediction. It has been noted that while some models are for group motion, others are for atomic movements. In addition, some models are restricted to some pathways while others allow the mobile station to move freely in any direction. Many setbacks of the current mobility prediction modes have been identified. Based on these shortcomings, a novel mobility prediction model has been proposed with some key requirements so that the proposed mobility prediction model can be as realistic as possible. The implementation of the proposed novel mobility prediction model is therefore recommended so as to address the GSM evils such as network outages due to inability to correctly locate a mobile station so that an incoming calls or data services can be delivered to it.

REFERENCES

Aarti M., Tracy C., & Nils A. (2012).Changing Trends in Modeling Mobility. *Journal of Electrical and Computer Engineering.* Volume 2012. (pp. 1-16).

Abdou A., Matrawy A., & Paul V. (2015). Accurate One-Way Delay Estimation with Reduced Client-Trustworthiness. IEEE Communications Letters.

Adebiyi S., Oyatoye E., & and Amole B. (2015).Modeling the Switching Behavior of Multiple-SIM GSM Subscribers in Nigeria Using Markov Chain Analysis. *The IUP Journal of Operations Management.* Vol 14(1). (pp.1-32).

Ahmad B. (2016). Hybrid fuzzy social mobility model. *Karbala International Journal of Modern Science.* Vol. 2(1). (pp. 29-40).

Biju I., Khairuddin H., & Tan C. (2010). Hybrid Mobility Prediction Of 802.11 Infrastructure Nodes By Location Tracking And Data Mining. *Journal of IT in Asia.* Vol (3). (pp. 9-24).

Chuyen L., Son D., Hyukro P., & Deokjai C. (2014). Mobility Prediction Algorithms Using User Traces in Wireless Networks. *Journal of Korea Multimedia Society.* Vol. 17, No. 8. (pp. 946-952).

Daniel H., Carolin T., Peter M., David W., Oliver H., Stefan R., André B. (2016). A hybrid and multiscale approach to model and simulate mobility in the context of public events. *International Scientific Conference on Mobility and Transport Transforming Urban Mobility.* Vol.(19). (pp. 350-363).

Fabrício A., Azzedine B., Thais R., Linnyer B., & Antonio A. (2015).A novel macroscopic mobility model for vehicular networks. *The International Journal of Computer and Telecommunications Networking.* Vo. 79(C). (pp. 188-202).

Garud V., More S., & Panpatil A. (2015). Mobility Location Prediction: A review of Techniques used in Mobile Ad-Hoc Network. *Journal of Electronics and Communication Engineering.* (pp. 59-68).

Hala A. (2015).Mobility Prediction in Dynamic Grids. Academia Education.

Jaswant S., & Rajneesh N. (2016). Improve Routing Efficiency Based on Mobility Models in Mobile Ad hoc Network. *International Journal of Advanced Research in Computer Science and Software Engineering*. Vol.6 (7). (pp. 512-519).

Joanne T. (2014).A Taxonomy and Survey of Microscopic Mobility Models from the Mobile Networking Domain. *ACM Computing Surveys (CSUR)*.Vol 47(1).

Jogendra K., & Panda M. (2016). Ad hoc network routing protocols on random waypoint model. *IEEE*.

Kim B., Kyong H., & Ki-Il K. (2017).A Survey on Mobility Support in Wireless Body Area Networks.*MDPI*. (pp.1-18).

Logambal R. & Chitra K. (2016). Mobility models and their influence on mobile AdHoc Networks. *Journal of Chemical and Pharmaceutical Sciences*. Vol 9(4). (pp. 1930-1934).

Mahmoud A., Ghaith H. & Wail M. (2016).Improving Vertical Handoffs Using Mobility Prediction. *International Journal of Advanced Computer Science and Applications*. Vol. 7(3). (pp 413-419).

Mariano G., André P., Michele T., & Ciro C. (2016). Predicting human mobility through the assimilation of social media traces into mobility models. *Springer Open Journal*. (pp. 1-15).

Martin L., Gudrun W., Rita C., Anita G., Johannes S., & Eva H. (2016). GIS and Transport Modeling—Strengthening the Spatial Perspective. *International Journal of Geo-Information*. (pp. 1-23).

Mona M., Morteza R., Hamideh B. (2015). The Impact of Mobility Prediction on the Performance of P2P Content Discovery Protocols over Mobile Ad-Hoc Networks. *Journal of Advances in Computer Research*. Vol. 6, No. 2. (pp. 45-64).

Mostafa K. (2016). User(s) Mobility Prediction in Mobile Networks to Enhance Location Based Services (LBS) Performance. *Universitat Bern*. (pp. 1-25).

Nandeppanavar A., Birje M., Manvi S., & Shridhar (2010). Mobility Impact on Performance of Mobile Grids. *International Journal of Computer Science and Information Security. Vol. 7.* (pp.106-111).

Nweke F., Anyigor S., and R. Iwu R.(2015). Mobility Management Scheme for Mobile Communication Systems: A Review. *IOSR Journal of Electronics and Communication Engineering (IOSR-JECE)*.Volume 10, Issue 6. (pp. 71-76*)*.

Patle V., & Sanjay K. (2016). Evaluation of Mobility Model with MANET Routing Protocols. *International Journal of Computer Applications*. Volume 152 – No.8. (pp. 8-12).

Petteri N. (2016). Modeling Mobility.*University of Helsinki*. (pp. 1-47).

Rogerio T., & Roberto R. (2016). BETA random waypoint mobility model for wireless network simulation. *The ACM Digital Library*.

Rong-Hua L., Jeffrey X., Lu Q., Rui M., & Tan J. (2015). On Random Walk Based Graph Sampling. *ICDE Conference*. (pp. 927-938).

Swati V., & Hina H. (2014).Comparison of Single Source Shortest Path Algorithms using C#. *3rd International Conference on System Modeling & Advancement in Research Trends*. (pp. 183-187).

Tao D., Xian W., Pingzhi F., &d Keqin L. (2016). Modeling and Performance Analysis of a Tracking-Area-List-Based Location Management Scheme in LTE Networks. *IEEE Transactions On Vehicular Technology*.VOL. 65, NO. 8. (pp. 6417-6431).

Tarik T., Abdelhakim H., & Apollinaire N. (2011).Mobility-Aware Streaming Rate Recommendation System. *Proceedings of IEEE Globecom*.

Yi-Bing L., Ming-Feng C., & Chien-Chun H. (2011).Derivation of Cell Residence Times from the Counters of Mobile Telecommunications Switches. *IEEE Transactions On Wireless Communications*. Vol. 10, No. 12. (pp. 4048-4051).

YOUR KNOWLEDGE HAS VALUE

- We will publish your bachelor's and
  master's thesis, essays and papers

- Your own eBook and book -
  sold worldwide in all relevant shops

- Earn money with each sale

Upload your text at www.GRIN.com
and publish for free